Supporting
Literacy

FOR AGES 7–8

Andrew Brodie

Introduction

Supporting Literacy is aimed at all those who work with children who have been identified as needing 'additional' or 'different' literacy support. It can be used by anyone working with children who fall into this category, whether you are a teacher, classroom assistant or parent.

Typically the seven to eight-year olds for whom this book is intended will be working at the levels expected of Year 1 and Year 2 children or they may simply need extra help in tackling the standard of work expected of Year 3. Their difficulties may be short term, and overcome with extra practice and support on a one to one or small group basis, or they may be long term where such support enables them to make progress but at a level behind their peer group. The activities in this book provide exactly what these children need – plenty of repetition and practice of basic skills, often covering the same ground but in a slightly different way. For this reason, you might decide to use the worksheets in a different order or just select the sheets that are suitable for the child or group of children you are working with. All the activities can be used on their own or alongside other literacy schemes that are already established within your school.

The worksheets are simple and self-explanatory and the instruction text is deliberately kept to a minimum to make the pages easy for adults to use and less daunting for children to follow. At the bottom of each page 'Notes for teachers' summarise the purpose of the activity and the learning target that is being addressed. Suggestions for additional activities are included if appropriate.

Most of the worksheets are based upon the National Literacy Strategy (NLS) objectives but some, where possible and relevant, are linked to other aspects of the curriculum. Through many years of experience of working with special needs children, the authors have been able to select the areas that these children find most difficult and provide useful activities that specifically address these stumbling blocks. Accordingly, and as set out below, most of the worksheets are centred around the word level strand of the Literacy Strategy.

The main targets addressed in this book are:
- Learning to read all the NLS high frequency words for Y1 and Y2
- Learning to spell some of these high frequency words
- Writing the days of the week and the months of the year
- Revising KS1 phonics:

  (1) ai, ee, ie, oa, oo, or, ar, ir, oi, ou
  (2) ay, a-e, ea, igh, y, i-e, o-e, oe, oy, ow, aw, air, ear, oo
- Counting syllables in a word and knowing that each syllable has a vowel (or y)
- Understanding the terms 'vowel' and 'consonant'
- Using picture and context clues to help decode text
- Self-correcting when reading if it doesn't make sense
- Reading with attention to commas and full stops
- Proof reading written work and spotting mis-spelt words
- Knowing alphabetical order and using this to locate words in a dictionary
- Writing sentences unaided, with prompts, using capital letters and full stops
- Adding question marks to questions
- Understanding other uses of capitals: pronoun 'I', names, headings, book titles

However you decide to use these sheets and in whatever context, it is worth remembering that children generally achieve the greatest success in an atmosphere of support and encouragement. Praise from a caring adult can be the best reward for children's efforts. The worksheets and activities in this book will provide many opportunities for children to enjoy their successes. The resulting increase in self-esteem will make a difference to their school work and other areas of school life too.

Individual record sheet

Name:

Worksheet	Teaching and learning objective	Target achieved	Needs more practice
1–2	To read words containing **oo**		
3–4	To read words containing final **e**		
5–6	To read words ending with **ear**		
7–8	To read words containing **ai**		
9–10	To recognise the phoneme **oa** (as in boat)		
11	To recognise the phoneme **oi**		
12	To recognise the phonemes **oy** and **ay**		
13–15	To recognise **ou** as in pound		
16	To spell the words **when what where** and **who** and read them in context		
17–18	To recognise that **ow** can be as in now or as in snow		
19	To recognise the vowel digraph **oe**		
20	To recognise and use the vowel phonemes **ar** and **ir**		
21	To recognise the vowel digraph **ie**		
22–23	To recognise and read **ight** in words		
24–25	To split compound words into their component parts		
26–27	To understand the terms vowel and consonant		
28–29	To be able to recognise syllables within words		
30–31	To check work for sense and make corrections		
32–33	To identify and correct mis-spelt words		
34	To learn to spell the days of the week		
35	To learn to read the months of the year		
36–37	To learn the order of the alphabet		
38	To learn to make use of the alphabet to find words on a dictionary card		
39	To spell North, South, East and West; to find other words with the phonemes or, ou and ea and with the final blends th and st		
40–41	To read the words North, South, East and West and the names of the countries of the British Isles		
42	To read and answer questions; to write own address		
43	To read words appropriate to the Y3 science topic on teeth; to practise the phonemes oo, ee, ou, th, aw, u; to consider plurals:		
44–46	To write sentences demarcated by appropriate use of capital letters and full stops; to make use of a dictionary card to assist with spelling:		

Record and Review

Name: _____ Date of birth: _____

Teacher: _____ Class: _____

Support assistant: _____

Code of Practice stage: _____ Date targets set: _____

Target

1 _____

2 _____

3 _____

4 _____

Review

Target

1 _____

_____

_____ Target achieved? ☐ Date: _____

2 _____

_____

_____ Target achieved? ☐ Date: _____

3 _____

_____

_____ Target achieved? ☐ Date: _____

4 _____

_____

_____ Target achieved? ☐ Date: _____

Content of the worksheets

The activities in this book are based on 'tracking back' in the Literacy Strategy to provide appropriate materials for Year 3 pupils who need extra support. Each sheet features a main activity and most also contain a subsidiary activity: the 'garden path'.

The garden path, which appears in a variety of different guises, contains nine NLS high frequency words for reading practice. Each path introduces a new word and provides practice of several words that have appeared on previous paths. As a child reads each word successfully they can colour the appropriate shape on the path. This can also serve as a useful tool for recording a child's progress over a series of lessons.

Worksheets 1–23 feature common phonic blends, with **Worksheet 16** introducing the 'question words' that begin with the consonant digraph **wh**.

Worksheets 24 and 25 introduce compound words.

Worksheets 26–29 deal with vowels and syllables.

Worksheets 30–33 Pupils are encouraged to check work for mistakes within the activities.

Worksheets 34–35 focus on the spellings of days of the week and months of the year.

Worksheets 36–38 encourage further practice of alphabetical order and how to make use of this when checking the spellings of words.

Worksheets 39–43 are linked to some of the work that pupils can expect to cover in geography and science during Year 3.

Worksheets 44–46 consist of dictation activities, providing practice of writing sentences correctly.

Resource sheets A–D provide a useful resource, consisting of flashcards for vowels, consonants and the major phonic blends.

Pages 58–61 contain a complete reading test to ascertain pupils' knowledge of most of the high frequency words for Key Stage 1. Teachers are able to gain a percentage score for each pupil. The test can be repeated after several months to check pupils' progress.

Pages 63–64 can be used to create a personal dictionary card for each pupil. This can be used alongside activities in this book and might also prove useful within class lessons. These sheets are a valuable resource for children of all abilities.

Name: _____   Date: _____

Write the correct word under each picture.

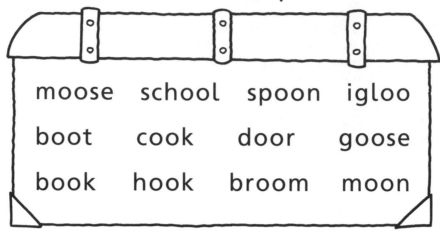

moose	school	spoon	igloo
boot	cook	door	goose
book	hook	broom	moon

- -

  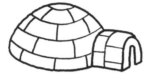  

- -

- -

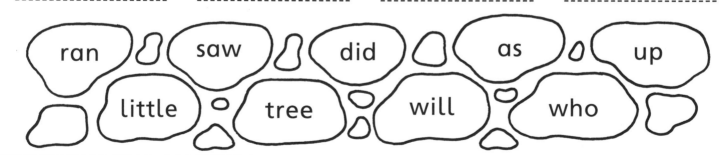

ran   saw   did   as   up

little   tree   will   who

Notes for teachers

Target: To read words containing **oo**

It's important to read the words through together before children start to match the words and pictures. Point out to them that the two letters **oo** can make different sounds in different words. Can they hear the difference between the phoneme **oo** as in spoon and the phoneme **u** as in book? You could also ask them to think of other words containing **oo**, e.g. soot, flood, blood, soon. Encourage correct letter formation when pupils are writing the words below the pictures. They can make simple sentences using the **oo** words, the garden path words and any other words the children know well.

Andrew Brodie: Supporting Literacy © A & C Black Publishers Ltd. 2006

Write the words from the box in
the correct sound sack.

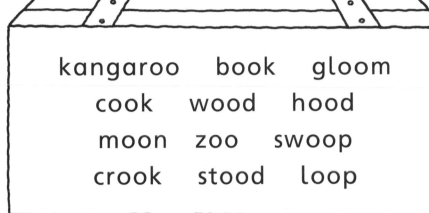

kangaroo   book   gloom
cook   wood   hood
moon   zoo   swoop
crook   stood   loop

look

----

boot

----

will   who   ran   saw   look
did   as   would   two

Notes for teachers
Target: To read words containing **oo**
Pupils should read the words from the box and should be encouraged to notice the differing sounds that the letters **oo**
can make. This sheet follows on from Worksheet 1. Encourage correct letter formation when pupils are writing the words
on the sacks. Ask pupils to use the 'oo' words in simple sentences. Support pupils in writing capital letters at the start of
sentences and full stops at the ends.

Name: _____   Date: _____

Write the correct word under each picture.

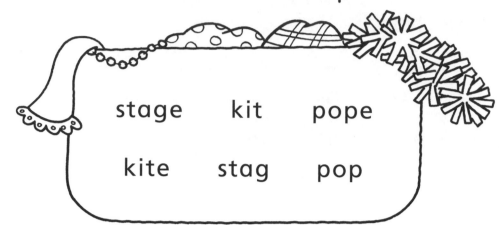

| stage | kit | pope |
| kite | stag | pop |

---------------------------   ---------------------------   ---------------------------

 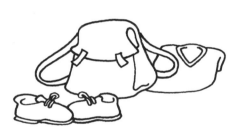 

---------------------------   ---------------------------   ---------------------------

would   two   will   who   ran

was   can't   next   like

Notes for teachers

Target: To read words containing final **e**

Explain to pupils that some words have a 'final e' at the end. This changes the sound of the earlier vowel from the letter sound to the letter name. Give some examples, e.g. pip to pipe, or sit to site. Encourage them to notice that the 'final e' changes the sound of the 'g' as well as the 'a' when comparing 'stag' and 'stage'. Ask them to write one or two of the sentences, making sure that each sentence starts with a capital letter and ends with a full stop.

Put the words in the correct places on the lines.
The first one has been done for you.

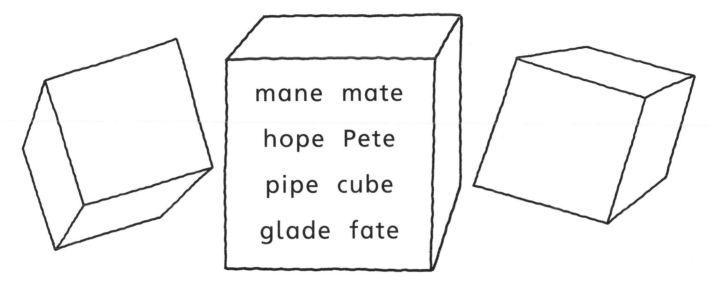

mane mate
hope Pete
pipe cube
glade fate

hop	____hope____	Now draw pictures for these words.
pip	------------------	
fat	------------------	
pet	------------------	
cub	------------------	
mat	------------------	
glad	------------------	
man	------------------	pin pine

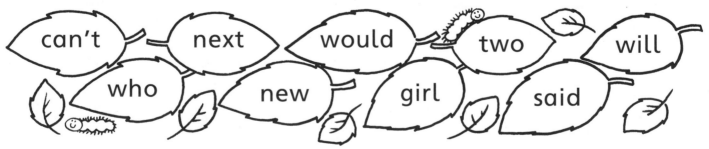

can't   next   would   two   will
who   new   girl   said

Name: _____ **Date:** _____

Read each word and copy it carefully.

ear

----

hear

----

fear

----

near

----

clear

----

rear

----

gear

----

spear

----

new   girl   can't   next   two

come   could   three   would

Notes for teachers

Target: To recognise words ending with **ear**

On this page it is important that pupils realise why the words are written within ears. Encourage pupils to make the words into sentences. This can be done orally or as a written task. As always, with any written work, ensure that each sentence starts with a capital letter and ends with a full stop.

Put the correct word with each picture,
then complete the sentences.

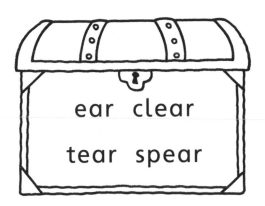

ear   clear

tear   spear

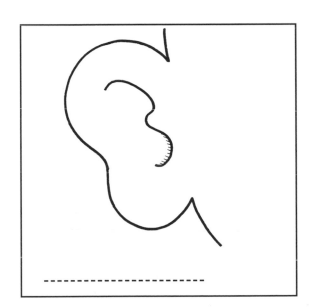

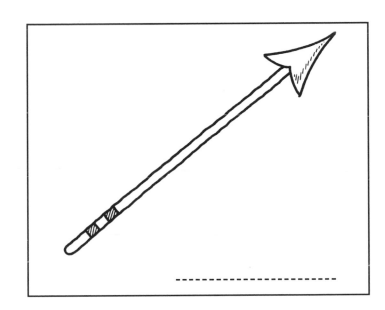

A _____ ran down her cheek.

Windows are _____ so you can see through them.

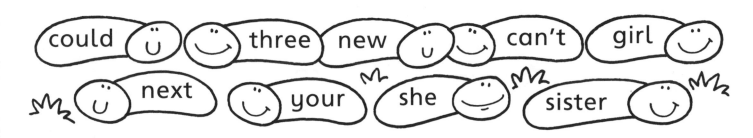

could   three   new   can't   girl

next   your   she   sister

Notes for teachers
Target: To recognise words ending in **ear**
This worksheet follows on from Worksheet 5. An added activity could be to put the words ear and spear in sentences.
As always, with any written work, ensure that each sentence starts with a capital letter and ends with a full stop.

Andrew Brodie: Supporting Literacy © A & C Black Publishers Ltd. 2006

Name: _____ Date: _____

Cut out the words and the pictures.
Stick the pictures into your book with
the correct words.

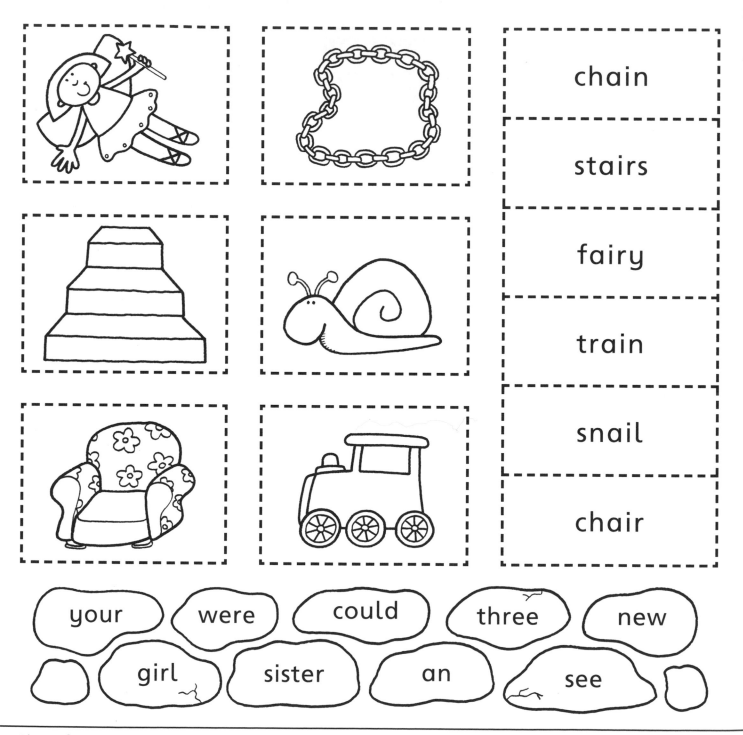

chain

stairs

fairy

train

snail

chair

your   were   could   three   new

girl   sister   an   see

Notes for teachers

Target: To read words containing **ai**

On this page the children are working with the phoneme **ai** (ay) and the phoneme **air**. Encourage the children to recognise the fact that the pair of letters **ai** appears in each word but that in some of the words the ai is combined with the letter **r**. Discuss the different sounds made in the two sets of words. Ask the pupils to stick the 'ai' words in one set and the 'air' words in another. Children should be encouraged to make up simple sentences containing each of the six words. This can be done orally or in writing.

Andrew Brodie: Supporting Literacy © A & C Black Publishers Ltd. 2006

Take words from the box and write them on the correct 'word snail'. The first two have been done for you.

WORD BANK

snail   fairy   drain   hair   mail   stair

air   rail   pair   plain   fair   aim

air

----

aim

----

were   an   your   sister   could

three   but   bed   yes

Notes for teachers

Target: To recognise the phonemes **ai** and **air** in words

As with Worksheet 7, it is important that children should be helped to hear the different sound in the words with **air** in them and those in which the **ai** makes the sound 'ay'. They should be encouraged to form letters correctly when copying the words. If there is time you could encourage pupils to make up sentences of their own using some of the words.

Read the words. Copy the words.
Draw a picture to go with each word.

goat	boat	moat

------------------------------- | ------------------------------- | -------------------------------

road	cloak	toad

------------------------------- | ------------------------------- | -------------------------------

but   bed   were   an   your

sister   got   over   ran

Notes for teachers
Target: To recognise the phoneme **oa** in words
Encourage children to form letters correctly when copying words. You could encourage the children to remember how to spell each word and write it – in this case you must focus on the **oa** being included in the memorised spellings.

Name: _____ **Date:** _____

Read the sentence. Colour the picture.

The goat on the boat
saw a toad on the road.

got   over   but   bed   were

an   her   pull   will

Notes for teachers

Target: To recognise the phoneme **oa** in words

Read the sentence with the children, encouraging them to understand the words by looking at the picture and observing 'the goat on the boat' and 'the toad on the road.' An additional activity would be to encourage children to make up their own silly sentence with 'oa' words and to illustrate it. As always, with any written work, ensure that each sentence starts with a capital letter and ends with a full stop.

Name: **Date:**

Use the words in the box to complete the sentences.
Colour the pictures.

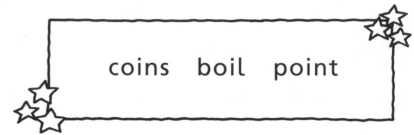

coins   boil   point

She counted

three ....

I can ....

to the stars.

The pan of water

can ....

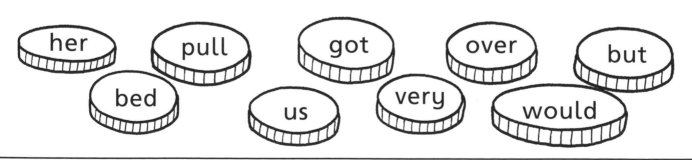

her   pull   got   over   but

bed   us   very   would

Notes for teachers

Target: To recognise the phoneme **oi**

Read the words with the children, stressing the phoneme **oi** (oy). Support them in reading the sentences and in identifying the missing word in each one. Help pupils to think of more 'oi' words, e.g. foil, coil, spoil. If there is time you could encourage pupils to make up sentences of their own using some of the words.

worksheet 12

Find the **oy** and **ay** words in the sentences.
Write them in the word sacks.

The boy gave hay to the horse.

Today you can play with the toys.

It may annoy me if you spray me
with cold water.

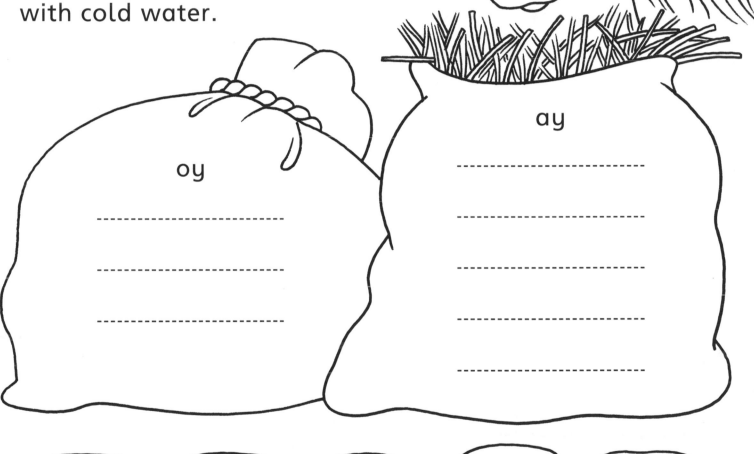

oy

----

ay

----

us   very   her   pull   got

over   love   must   can't

Notes for teachers
Target: To recognise the phonemes **oy** and **ay**
Support the pupils in reading the three sentences, then in looking for the 'ay' and 'oy' words. Encourage them to look very closely by asking questions. For example: Has every sentence on the sheet got an 'oy' word? Has every sentence on the sheet got an 'ay' word? Which sentence has more than one 'ay' word? Encourage children to think of additional words, eg. play, stay, destroy, ploy.

Name: _____ **Date:** _____

Copy the sentences and draw the pictures.

I found a round pound.

```
[empty box for drawing]
```

A hound was in the playground.

```
[empty box for drawing]
```

love   must   us   very   got

over   just   door   new

Notes for teachers

Target: To recognise **ou** as in pound

Encourage the children to find the rhyming words in each sentence. Stress the phoneme **ou** (ow) and point out that, in these words, it is spelt **ou**. Ask children to think of other words with an 'ow' sound. They will come up with correct answers that include words spelt with **ow** or **ou**, e.g. cow, out, about, how. Write each of the words enabling them to pick out the ones with **ou** in.

Read the poem. Underline the words with **ou** in them.

I looked up and saw a cloud.

"Oh look!" I shouted very loud,

"That cloud looks like a little mouse."

Then it rained on me and on my house.

just   door   where   us   must

could   when   love   very

Notes for teachers

Target: To recognise **ou** as in pound

Read the poem to the children several times. Encourage pupils to read the poem clearly and confidently themselves. Help them to find and underline the 'ou' words. Discuss the sound 'ou'. If there is time, you could encourage pupils to make up sentences of their own using some of the words.

Name: _____ **Date:** _____

Put the correct words with the pictures.

WORD BANK

trout   house   hound   cloud

mountain   shout   mouse   fountain

- - - - - - - - - - - - -   - - - - - - - - - - - - -   - - - - - - - - - - - - -   - - - - - - - - - - - - -

- - - - - - - - - - - - -   - - - - - - - - - - - - -   - - - - - - - - - - - - -   - - - - - - - - - - - - -

when   where   just   door   love

must   dig   put   your

Notes for teachers

Target: To recognise **ou** as in pound

Discuss the words with the children. Ask them which words rhyme with each other. Can they think of other words that rhyme with these? Look especially at mountain and fountain, pointing out the **ou** but also the **ai** in each word. Encourage children to use the 'ou' words in simple written sentences. As always, with any written work, ensure that each sentence starts with a capital letter and ends with a full stop.

Name: **Date:**

Read and write these sentences.

"Where did my dog go?"

"Who is going to play with me?"

"What are we going to do today?"

"When can we go out to play?"

Practise spelling these words.

when	what	where	who
-----------------	-----------------	-----------------	-----------------
-----------------	-----------------	-----------------	-----------------

Can you think of any more words that begin with 'wh'?

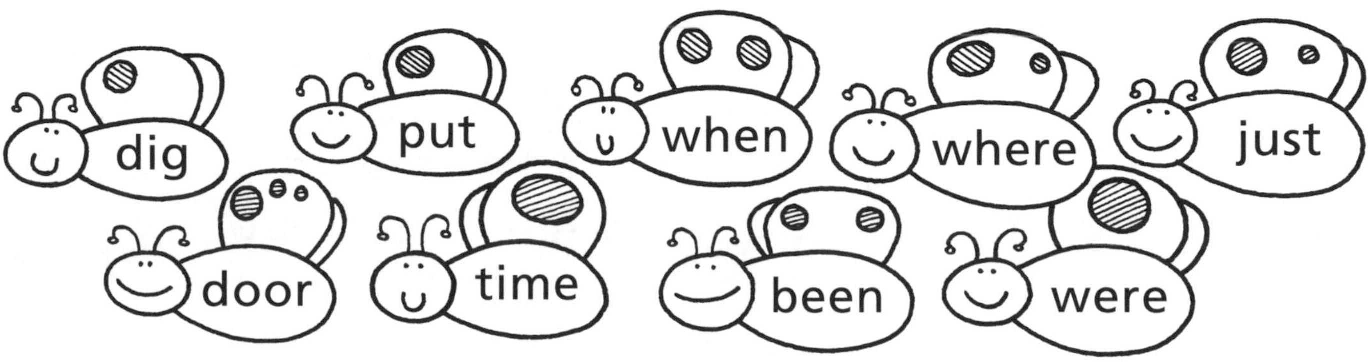

-----------------   -----------------   -----------------   -----------------

dig   put   when   where   just

door   time   been   were

Notes for teachers
Target: To spell the words **when**, **what**, **where** and **who** and read them in context
Children should have the question marks and speech marks pointed out to them, noticing that the question mark is
written before the closing speech marks. Focus on the **wh** beginning of each of the words for spelling. Encourage children
to think of more **wh** words, e.g. which, whether, white.

Name: _____ **Date:** _____

Match the words to the pictures.

```
WORD BANK
    cow   owl   clown   bungalow
    tower   crow   flower   bow
```

- -

- -

Draw an owl in a gown flying over a town.

time	been	dig	put	when

where	after	school	but

Notes for teachers
Target: To recognise that **ow** can be as in now or as in snow
Read the words with the children. Ensure they can hear the two different sounds made by the **ow** in these words.
For extra practice, they could rewrite the words on a separate piece of paper or in an exercise book sorting them into two
lists according to the sounds made by the digraph **ow**. The picture of 'the owl in a gown flying over a town' can be done
in a book or on a piece of paper.

Name: _____ **Date:** _____

Read the words. Write them on the correct word walls.

WORD BANK

flower   power   grow   brown   crow   cow   flow

crown   glow   now   slow   blow

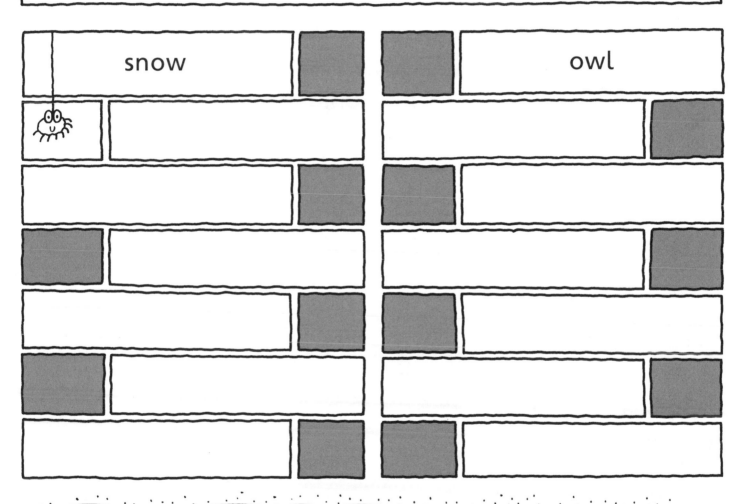

snow			owl

after   school   time   been   dig

put   do   by   got

Notes for teachers

Target: To recognise that **ow** can be as in now or as in snow

This worksheet follows on from Worksheet 17. An extension activity could be to find other 'ow' words and add them to the correct walls.

Name: _____   **Date:** _____

Read the words. Write them in the correct word sack.

WORD BANK

toes   goes

shoe   Joe

canoe

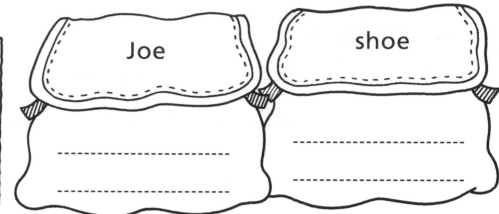

Joe

shoe

Read the sentence. Copy the sentence.

Joe goes for a ride in a canoe.

_____

do   by   after   school   time

been   ball   from   her

Notes for teachers

Target: To recognise the vowel digraph **oe**

By writing the vowel digraph **oe**, the pupils are practising the spelling of a common letter cluster. The word 'goes' is particularly relevant as it is one of the high frequency words identified in the NLS. Discuss the sounds made by **oe** in each of the words, encouraging the children to notice that the sound in canoe and shoe is **oo** and in the other words it is **oa**. You could ask the children to make up their own written sentence ensuring that they start the sentence with a capital letter and end it with a full stop.

Read the words. Write them in the correct circles.

WORD BANK

girl star car bird birthday birth

start cart shirt farm dirty shark

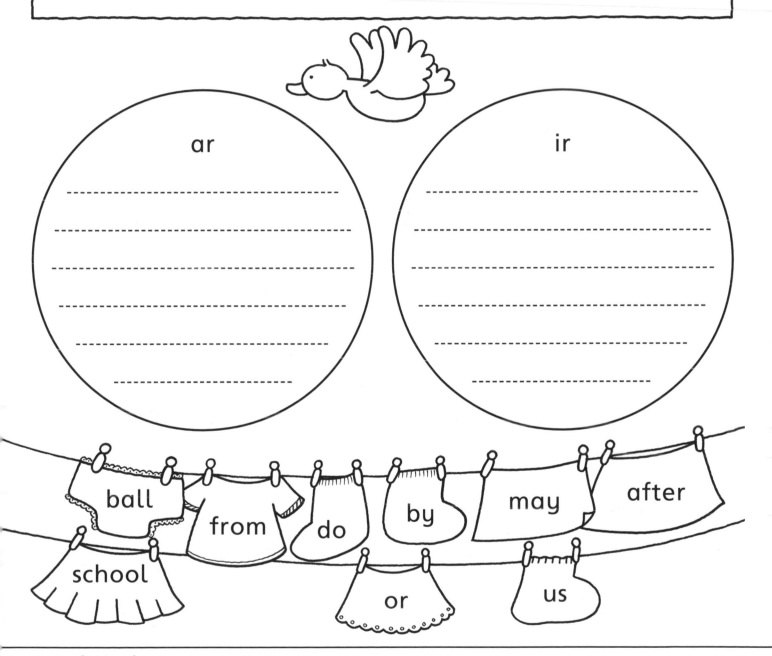

ar

----

ir

----

ball   from   do   by   may   after

school   or   us

Notes for teachers

Target: To recognise and use the vowel phonemes **ar** and **ir**

Help the children read the words in the box. Encourage them to observe the vowel/consonant digraphs **ar** and **ir** within the words. Help them to identify the different sounds (phonemes) made by the two digraphs, to enable them to copy the words into the correct circles. Note that the word 'birthday' appears before the word 'birth' as the children are more likely to recognise birthday. This will provide an opportunity to introduce compound words to the children. Show them that birthday is obviously a combination of birth and day and that it means the day of birth.

Name: **Date:**

Read the words.

WORD BANK

pie   lie   fries   cries   dried

Write a sentence for each one.

1. --

----

2. --

----

3. --

----

4. --

----

5. --

----

may   or   ball   from   do

because   by   love   back

Notes for teachers

Target: To recognise the vowel digraph **ie**

Help the children read the words. Ask them to say what is the same in each word: they may say that the sound 'ie' is the same in each word and they may say that each word contains 'i 'and 'e' together. The children may need some help in thinking of sentences and in writing them. Remind the children that each sentence needs a capital letter at the start and a full stop at the end.

Name: **Date:**

Read the sentence.
Draw a picture to go with it.

I had a fright in the middle of the night.

Notes for teachers
Target: To recognise and read **ight** in words
Encourage children to write the 'ight' words and to say the letters as they write them. Ask them to think of other words
with the same spelling pattern, e.g. might, light, fight, tight. They may also suggest the word high. Help them to think of
other sentences containing 'ight' words. You could write these out for them to read or ask them to write one or more
sentences of their own. As always, with any written work, ensure that each sentence starts with a capital letter and ends
with a full stop.
Andrew Brodie: Supporting Literacy © A & C Black Publishers Ltd. 2006

Name: _____   **Date:** _____

The pictures show different sorts of light.
Label the pictures.

┌─ **WORD BANK** ────────────────────────────────────┐

moonlight   firelight   streetlight   headlight

└──┘

- -

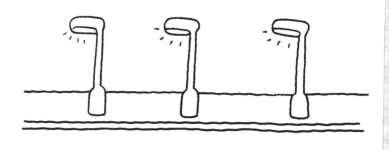

- -

- -

- -

Can you think of other sorts of light?

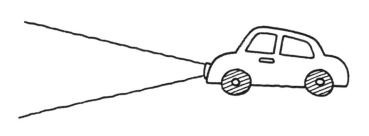

should   good   back   because   may   or   man   house   saw

Notes for teachers

Target: To recognise and read **ight** in words

Use this opportunity to introduce the idea of a word made from two shorter words and inform the children that these words are called compound words. Other types of light might include sunlight, candlelight, lamplight. Help the children to think of sentences using some of these words. Ask them to choose one of these sentences to write down. As always, with any written work, ensure that each sentence starts with a capital letter and ends with a full stop.

    Andrew Brodie: Supporting Literacy © A & C Black Publishers Ltd. 2006

Name: _____ **Date:** _____

Read these words.

   wind   post   spoon   ball   man   mill   tea   foot

Put two of the words together to make one word to go with each of the pictures.

--   --

--   --

man   house   should   good   back

because   way   make   who

Notes for teachers
Target: To split compound words into their component parts
Help the children read the words shown. Explain that they are going to combine some of the words to make new 'compound' words. Help pupils to think of more compound words, e.g. sunshine, sunglasses, moonlight. Support the children in thinking of sentences using some of these words, perhaps making use of some of the garden path words, eg. I may wear sunglasses when I am sitting in the sunshine. If the child is confident you could add an extra clause to the sentence: ... because the sun is so bright. Ask the child to choose one of these sentences to write down.

Andrew Brodie: Supporting Literacy © A & C Black Publishers Ltd. 2006

Name: _____   Date: _____

Read the words. Make the compound word and draw the picture. The first one has been done for you.

sun + shine	sunshine	
air + craft		
hill + side		

way   make   man   house   should

good   old   not   two

Notes for teachers

Target: To split compound words into their component parts

Ensure that letters are formed correctly when the children are writing the compound words. Support the children in thinking of sentences using some of these words. Ask the child to choose one of these sentences to write down.

Andrew Brodie: Supporting Literacy © A & C Black Publishers Ltd. 2006

Vowels are very important letters. They make you open your mouth when you say words.

The vowels are: **a e i o u**

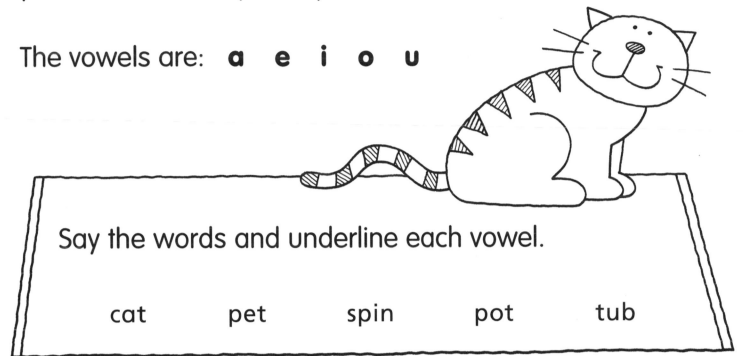

Say the words and underline each vowel.

cat   pet   spin   pot   tub

The letter y can act like a vowel.

Read these words.

fly   my   sty   cry

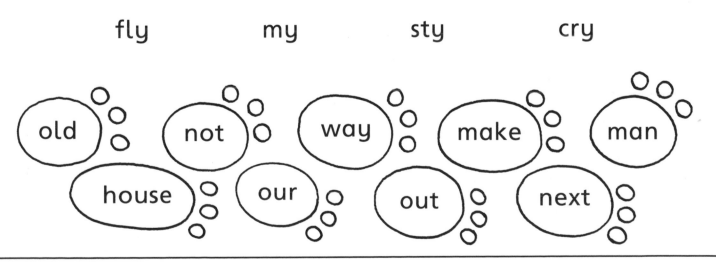

old   not   way   make   man

house   our   out   next

Notes for teachers
Target: To understand the terms vowel and consonant
Ask the children to try to say words with the vowels missing, e.g. mddle instead of muddle or mtl instead of metal. Use the terms 'vowel' and 'consonant'. Help the children think of sentences using some of the words, perhaps making use of some of the garden path words. Ask the child to choose one of these sentences to write down.

Look at the alphabet. Put a ring round the vowels and the letter y.

a b c d e f g h i j k l m n o p q r s t u v w x y z

Read the sentence. Underline the vowels.

I like to go fishing in the summer.

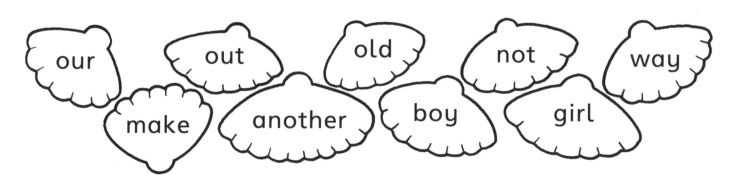

our   out   old   not   way

make   another   boy   girl

Notes for teachers
Target: To understand the terms vowel and consonant
Discuss the sentence with the children, ensuring that they understand what it means. Then discuss each word, supporting the children in identifying the vowels (including the capital letter I at the start of the sentence). Encourage the use of the terms vowels and consonants. Point out that every word in the sentence has at least one vowel, then discuss the fact that each syllable has a vowel, e.g. in the word fish – ing. Pupils may need to be reminded about syllables and may find it helpful to sound out their own names, identifying the syllables and vowels. More work is provided for this on Worksheet 25.

Name: **Date:**

Count the number of syllables in each of the words.
Write the number in the box.

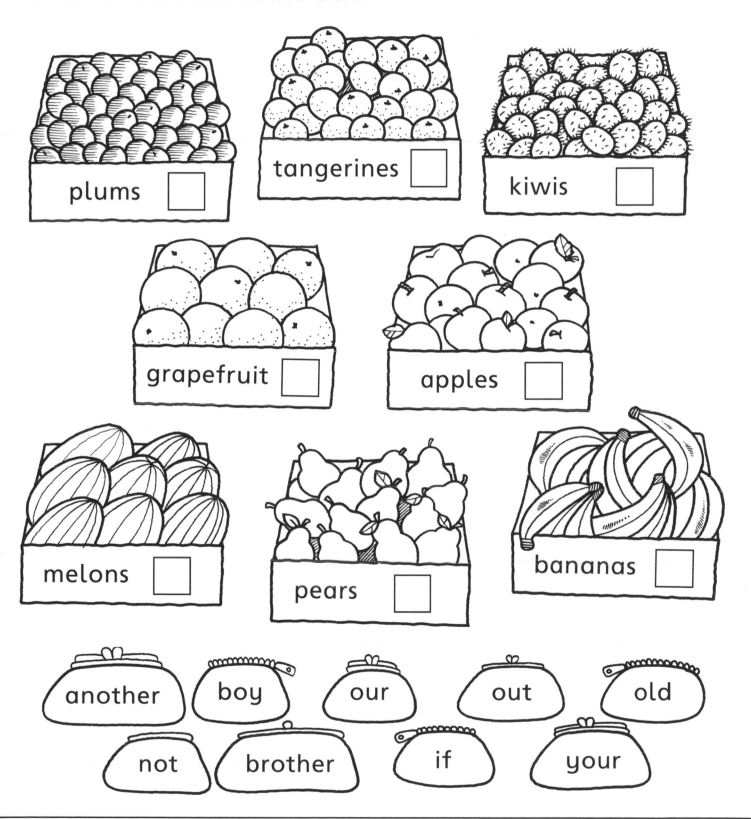

plums ☐

tangerines ☐

kiwis ☐

grapefruit ☐

apples ☐

melons ☐

pears ☐

bananas ☐

another   boy   our   out   old

not   brother   if   your

Notes for teachers
Target: To be able to recognise syllables within words
Before starting this work ensure children understand what a syllable is. One way to do this is for pupils to say their names
and clap the syllables as they are said.

Name: _____

Date: _____

Look at the animals. Read their names.
How many syllables are in each name?

tiger ☐   elephant ☐   giraffe ☐

kangaroo ☐   horse ☐   hippopotamus ☐

brother   if   another   boy   our

out   jump   push   sister

Notes for teachers

Target: To be able to recognise syllables within words

This worksheet continues the work covered on Worksheets 24 and 25. As an extension activity, ask the children to think of as many animals as they can with 1 syllable, 2 syllables, then 3 syllables. You could draw a simple table, headed '1 syllable', etc, then write the words in the appropriate columns with the children. Note that some words will be single syllable words but will have more than one vowel, e.g. goat. Here the two vowels **o** and **a** are forming the vowel digraph **oa**.

Each sentence has one silly word in it.
Choose a word from the box to make the
sentence sensible.

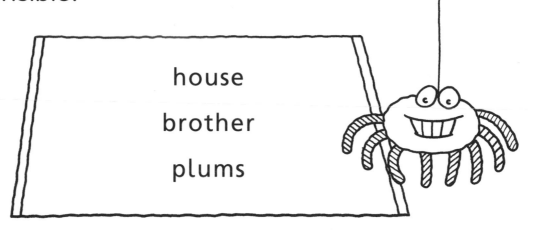

house

brother

plums

Write the correct sentences.

Ben lived in a horse.

I like to eat plugs.

My little sister is called Tom.

an   push   jump   be   if

another   brother   about   boy

Notes for teachers
Target: To check work for sense and make corrections
Read the sentences with the children and discuss the errors with them before they do the written part of the task.
As always, with any written work, ensure that each sentence starts with a capital letter and ends with a full stop.

Ring the word that makes sense in each of
the sentences.

My (fresh fender friend) likes to play with me.

Ben's new jumper
is (reed red rub).

The sleeve of my
(shirt skirt scarf)
was torn.

be	about	brother	if	push
take	some	jump	but	

Notes for teachers
Target: To check writing for sense and make corrections
Support the children in reading the sentences. The words in brackets can cause great confusion and the children will need
to understand that they are simply choosing the correct word from the three provided. They could attempt to read each
sentence using each of the three words so that they can 'hear' which version makes sense. You could invent other similar
sentences where the choice of words only varies by one or two letters.

36   Andrew Brodie: Supporting Literacy © A & C Black Publishers Ltd. 2006

Name: **Date:**

Each sentence has some words that have been
spelt wrongly.
Use your word book or a dictionary to help you to
write each sentence correctly.

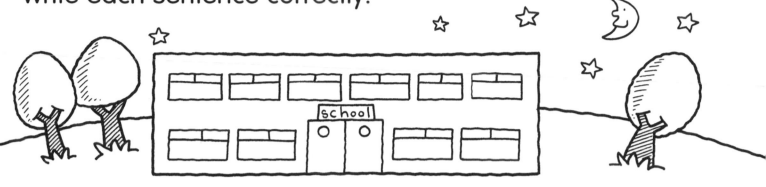

The skool is not open at nite.

"Go owt to play," sed dab.

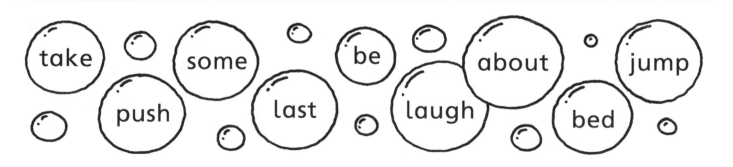

Notes for teachers
Target: To identify and correct mis-spelt words
Discuss the mistakes in the sentences before tackling the written element of the task. Pupils may need help to use a word
book or dictionary correctly. This is an important skill that they should be helped to develop. You may wish to make use of
the dictionary card that can be created from pages 63 and 64 of this book.

Each sentence has some words that have been wrongly spelt.
Use your word book or a dictionary to help you to write each sentence correctly.

Thay wer going up the rowd.

Wee can gow to skool today.

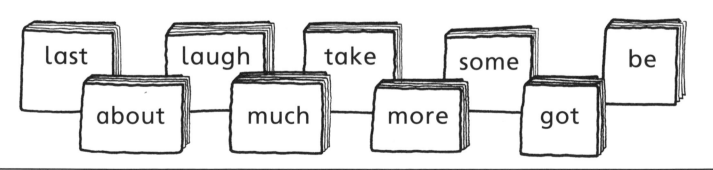

last   laugh   take   some   be

about   much   more   got

Notes for teachers
Target: To identify and correct mis-spelt words
You could extend the activity by making sentences of your own for pupils to correct. Make a point of using your pupils' common spelling errors when doing this. Ensure that the children write the sentences using capital letters and full stops as appropriate.

worksheet 34

Tuesday Friday Monday Saturday

Wednesday Sunday Thursday

Write the days in the correct order. We have written Monday for you.

_____ Monday _____

_____

_____

_____

_____

What day is it today?

_____

What day will it be tomorrow?

_____

much   more   last   laugh   take

some   call   once   over

Notes for teachers

Target: To learn to spell the days of the week and to answer questions about the order of the days; to write the first letter of each day's name with a capital letter; to write a set of sentences with some prompts.

You may wish to allow the children to use the back of the dictionary card that can be made using pages 63 and 64 of this book. Many children in Year 3 find spelling the days of the week quite difficult, particularly Wednesday. It can help them to break the words up, e.g. Wed nes day. Remind the child that days of the week are special words and need capital letters at the start. Ask questions about what happens on certain days. For example, you could ask the child what he/she does on a Saturday. They could then write a sentence about this, on a separate piece of paper. If there is time you could encourage the child to write a sentence about each day. By dealing with each day separately and giving lots of praise and encouragement you could achieve a set of seven sentences.

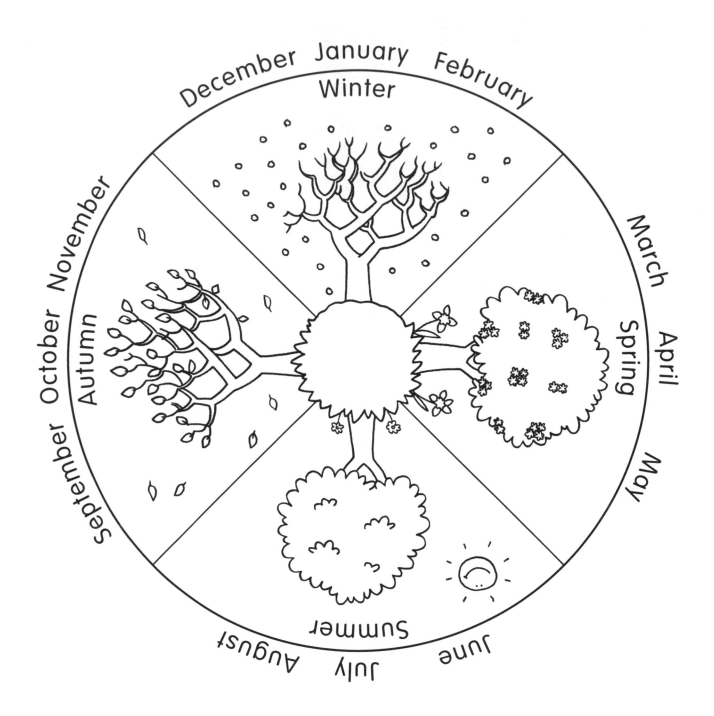

Notes for teachers

Target: To learn to read the months of the year and to answer questions about them; to write the first letter of each month's name with a capital letter; to write a set of sentences with some prompts.

Read the months with the child, turning the sheet round so that the name of the month is level when the child reads it. Discuss which months come in each season. Discuss the current month and the current season. Encourage the child to identify features of the season and perhaps events that take place that month. Ask questions about what happens in certain months. For example, ask the child in which month his/her birthday takes place. If the child doesn't know the answer, take him/her to look at the school register to find out – he/she needs to know! You could tell the child which month your birthday occurs in.

Name: _____   **Date:** _____

Join the dots. Write one word for each letter.

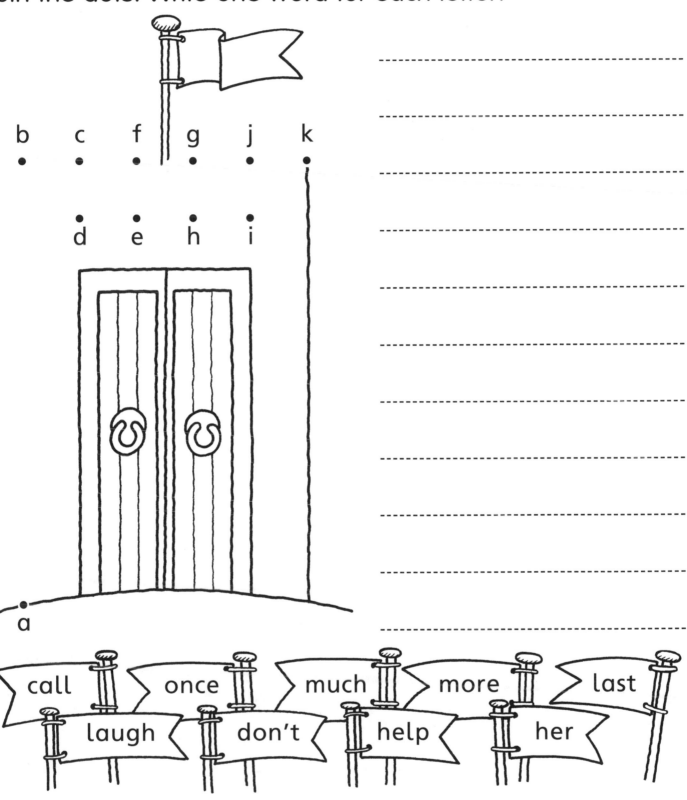

b   c   f   g   j   k

d   e   h   i

a

call   once   much   more   last

laugh   don't   help   her

Notes for teachers

Target: To learn the order of the alphabet

Many children in Year 3 still find the order of the alphabet difficult to remember. This worksheet provides practice of the alphabet as far as letter k. Worksheet 37 provides practice from l to z. We have split the alphabet at this point as some children who have learnt the well-known alphabet rhyme find the section l, m, n, o, p the hardest part. Encourage the children to think of a word for each letter and support them in writing the words. You may like to make use of the dictionary card made from pages 63 and 64.

Name: **Date:**

Join the dots.

Write one word for each letter.

```
----------------------------    ----------------------------    ----------------------------

----------------------------    ----------------------------    ----------------------------

----------------------------    ----------------------------    ----------------------------

----------------------------    ----------------------------    ----------------------------

----------------------------    ----------------------------    ----------------------------
```

don't   help   call   once   much

more   then   too   pull

Notes for teachers

Target: To learn the order of the alphabet

Many children in Year 3 still find the order of the alphabet difficult to remember. This worksheet provides practice of the alphabet from l to z. Worksheet 36 provides practice from a to k. We have split the alphabet at this point as some children who have learnt the well-known alphabet rhyme find the section l, m, n, o, p the hardest part. Encourage the children to think of a word for each letter and support them in writing the words. You may like to make use of the dictionary card made from pages 63 and 64.

Look at the dictionary card and answer these questions.

What is the first letter of the alphabet?

What is the last letter of the alphabet?

How many words are written under letter b?

How many words are written under letter h?

Which letters on the card only have one word?

Which letter on the card has the most words?

Notes for teachers
Target: To learn to make use of the alphabet; to find words on a dictionary Dary card
To complete this worksheet the child will need to make use of the dictionary card made from pages 63 and 64. Discuss the card with the child showing him/her that the words on the front of the card are in alphabetical order and that the words on the back include the names of the days of the week, the months of the year, colours, etc. If possible the child should keep a copy of the dictionary card for use in class. Support the child in answering the questions on this worksheet. You could make up similar questions about other letters, perhaps doing these together before the child attempts to answer the questions on this sheet.

Name: _____   **Date:** _____

Write the correct word for each compass point.

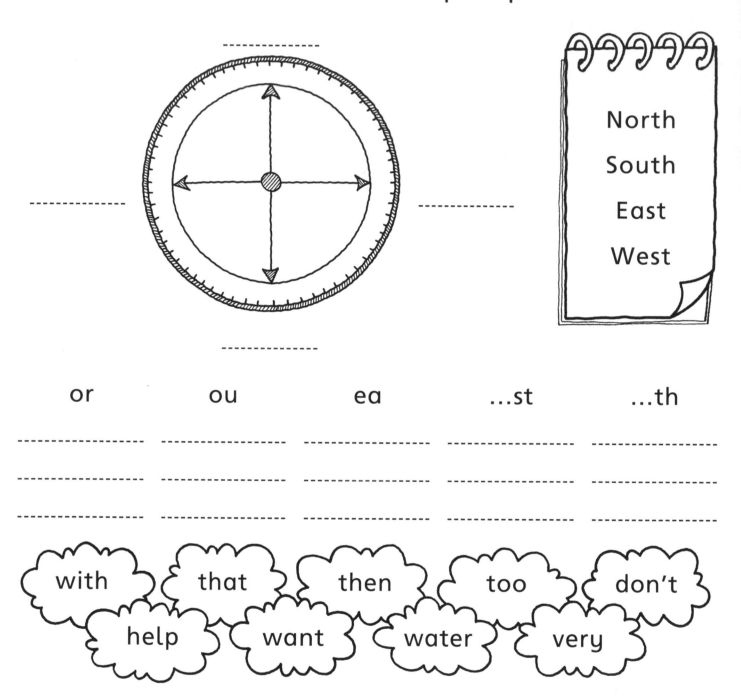

North

South

East

West

or	ou	ea	...st	...th
----------------	----------------	----------------	----------------	----------------
----------------	----------------	----------------	----------------	----------------
----------------	----------------	----------------	----------------	----------------

with   that   then   too   don't

help   want   water   very

Notes for teachers

Target: To spell North, South, East and West; to find other words with the phonemes **or**, **ou** and **ea** and with the final blends th and st. This sheet links to work that pupils cover in Year 3, regarding compass directions.

Discuss the positions of North, South, East and West and help the child write them in the correct places . If possible, consider the positions in relation to the school. Now discuss the word 'North'. Ask the child what sound it starts with, what sound is in the middle and what sound it ends with, then to write it in the 'or' list. Can the child think of any other words that have the sound 'or'? You could suggest examples: fort, for, torch, porch. You may find that the child will suggest other words with the phoneme **or** but that are spelt differently; for example, bought, caught, etc. Congratulate him/her for correctly identifying the sound but do not let him/her write the words in the 'or' list as only words spelt that way should be entered. Instead, write the words on a separate piece of paper so that he/she can observe that the sound can be spelt in different ways in some words. Work with the other sounds in similar ways. With **ou** the child should only write words on the list that that have the same sound and spelling; eg, out, about, mouth. Similarly with **ea**; eg, eat, meat, feast (but not head or bread).

Name: _____ **Date:** _____

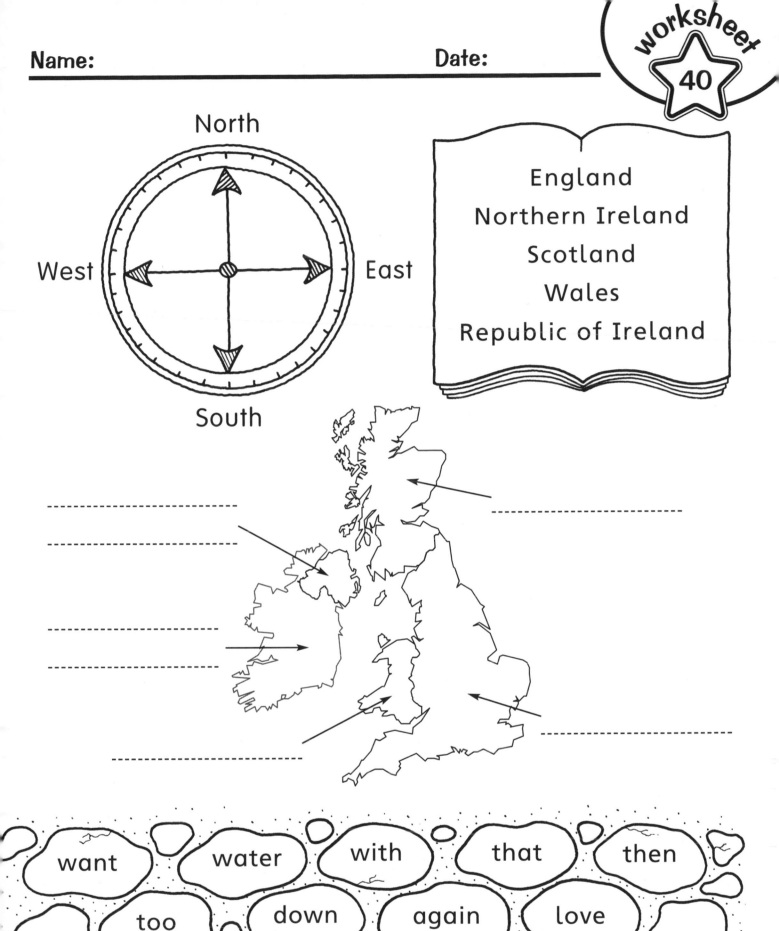

North

West   East

South

England
Northern Ireland
Scotland
Wales
Republic of Ireland

- - - - - - - - - - - - - - - -

- - - - - - - - - - - - - - - -

- - - - - - - - - - - - - - - -

- - - - - - - - - - - - - - - -

- - - - - - - - - - - - - - - -

- - - - - - - - - - - - - - - -

want   water   with   that   then

too   down   again   love

Notes for teachers

Target: To read the words North, South, East and West and the names of the countries of the British Isles; to answer questions and to pose questions, making appropriate use of question marks.

This sheet links to work that pupils cover in Year 3, regarding places. The sheet can be used in conjunction with Worksheet 39. Remind the child of the compass directions. Support him/her in reading the names of the countries and in writing these in the correct places. You could point out that England, Ireland and Scotland all end with the word 'land'.

Name:

Date:

Look at the map on Worksheet 40.

Which country is east of Wales?

Which country is west of England?

Write two questions of your own.

1. --

   ----

2. --

   ----

that again her came down here water want with

Notes for teachers

Target: To read the words North, South, East and West and the names of the countries of the British Isles; to answer questions and to pose questions, making appropriate use of question marks.

This sheet links to work that pupils cover in Y3 Geography, regarding places. The sheet should be used in conjunction with Worksheet 40. Remind the child of the compass directions. Support him/her in reading the questions and in finding the answers. Discuss the fact that questions are sentences with question marks at the end instead of full stops. Assist him/her in writing some questions, e.g. Which country is south of Scotland? Which country is north of England? Which country is west of Scotland? (Pointing out that Northern Ireland is west of part of Scotland.) Discuss the fact that the countries need capital letters because they are names (proper nouns).

Andrew Brodie: Supporting Literacy © A & C Black Publishers Ltd. 2006

Do you live in a street or a road or a village?

Which street, road or village do you live in?

Do you live in a town or near a town?

Which town?

Which county do you live in?

Can you write your address?

came   here   down   again   want

water   made   off   must

Notes for teachers
Target: To read and answer questions; to write own address.
This sheet links to work that pupils cover in Year 3 Geography. Support the child in reading the questions and in finding the answers. Discuss the fact that questions are sentences with question marks at the end instead of full stops. Remind the child that place names always start with capital letters. Encourage him/her to write full sentences to answer the questions. For example: I live in a village. My village is called ... Assist the child in writing his/her own address.

Name: _____ **Date:** _____

Can you read these words?

tooth   teeth   mouth   jaw   jaws   gum   gums

Can you think of more words for these lists?

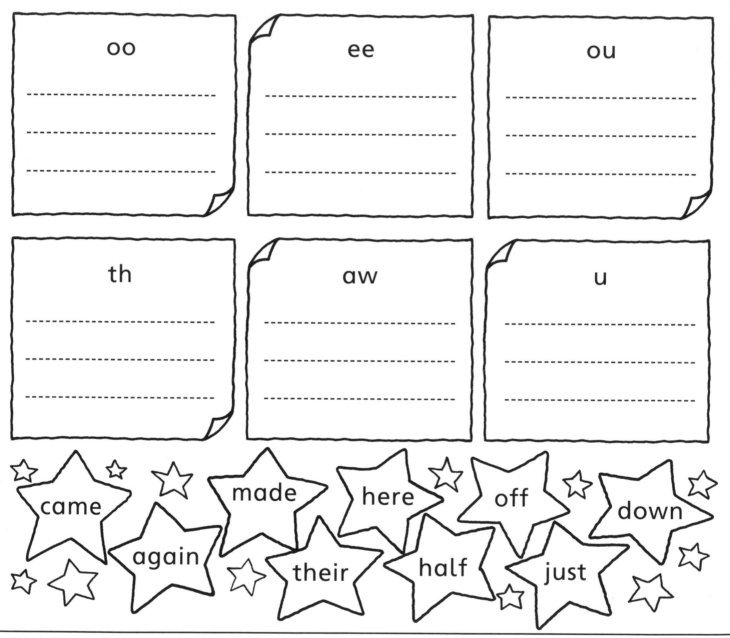

oo	ee	ou
-------------	-------------	-------------
-------------	-------------	-------------
-------------	-------------	-------------

th	aw	u
-------------	-------------	-------------
-------------	-------------	-------------
-------------	-------------	-------------

came   again   made   their   here   half   off   just   down

Notes for teachers

Target: To read words appropriate to the Year 3 Science topic on teeth; to practise the phonemes **oo, ee, ou, th, aw, u**; to consider plurals.

This sheet links to Science work that pupils cover in Year 3. Support the child in reading the words. Discuss the fact that they are all words connected with the mouth. Ensure that the child understands what the jaws and gums are. Support him/her in finding more words for the lists. For example: **oo**: boot, root, shoot (but not book or look as the sound is different); **ee**: feet, sheet, keep; **ou**: south, out, about, shout, ground; **th**: south, path, moth; **aw**: claw, paw, saw; **u**: but, put, sum.

Discuss the fact that jaws is the plural of jaw and that plural means more than one. Lots of plurals are made by adding s. But now look at **teeth**; this is the plural of **tooth** and this time the middle has changed. Can they think of another word that changes in the same way to make the plural? (foot, feet)

Notes for teachers

The next three worksheets are to be used for pupils to write sentences unaided. The children can make use of the dictionary card that can be made from pages 63 and 64 of this book.

Each worksheet will feature a dictation exercise that an adult will read out loud to the children. The adult may need to allow time for the children to make use of their dictionary card.

The first exercise consists of short, simple sentences. In the second exercise the sentences include the need to write capital letters for names and for a book title. The third exercise includes speech marks and question marks.

You will need to read each sentence several times, offering lots of encouragement to the pupils and allowing them time to look up spellings on the dictionary card made from pages 63 and 64 of this book. Remind pupils that each sentence starts with a capital letter and ends with a full stop.

Dictation exercise 1

I have a dog at home.

My dog is black and white.

My dog likes to bark.

I love my dog.

Dictation exercise 2

In my school there is a teacher called Mrs ....

Mrs .... likes to read to her class.

She is reading a book called *The Very Hungry Caterpillar*.

Dictation exercise 3

"What is your name?" asked Mr Brown.

"My name is Jenny," said the girl.

their   half   made   off   came

here   first   one   door

Notes for teachers

Target: To write sentences demarcated by appropriate use of capital letters and full stops. To make use of a dictionary card to assist with spelling.

This is dictation exercise 1 (please refer to page 49). The exercise consists of four simple sentences containing mainly words from the NLS list of high frequency words for KS1, plus the words 'likes' and 'bark'.

first   one   their   half   made

off   live   there   when

Notes for teachers

Target: To write sentences demarcated by appropriate use of capital letters and full stops. To use capital letters for names and for book titles. To make use of a dictionary card to assist with spelling.

This is dictation exercise 2 (please refer to page 49). The exercise consists of three simple sentences containing mainly words from the NLS list of high frequency words for KS1, plus the words 'teacher', 'read', 'reading', 'book', 'hungry' and 'caterpillar' and the abbreviated word 'Mrs'. Use the name of a teacher in your own school at the appropriate points in sentences 1 and 2.

Name:

Date:

$4 + 2 =$

live   there   first   one   their

half   what   now   where

Notes for teachers

Target: To write sentences demarcated by appropriate use of capital letters and full stops; to use capital letters for names; to add question marks to sentences; to begin to use speech marks; to make use of a dictionary card to assist with spelling. This is dictation exercise 3 (please refer to page 49). The exercise consists of two sentences containing mainly words from the NLS list of high frequency words for KS1, plus the words 'asked', 'Brown' and 'Jenny' and the abbreviated word 'Mr.' The punctuation of these sentences is much more complicated than the punctuation of the previous two exercises. You may like to show the pupils the written sentences before dictating them. Point out the use of speech marks; show them the question mark in the first sentence that must be placed before the closing speech marks of Mr Brown's question; show them the comma in the second sentence that must be placed before the closing speech marks of the girl's reply. Remind pupils that people's names need initial capitals.

Andrew Brodie: Supporting Literacy © A & C Black Publishers Ltd. 2006

Vowels

a	e	i	o	u

Consonants

b	c	d	f	g	h
j	k	l	m	n	p
q	r	s	t	v	w
x	y	z			

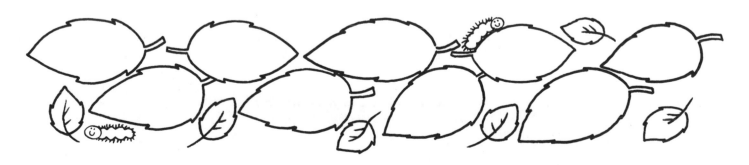

Double consonant endings

ff	ll	ss	ck	ng

Double consonant endings

ld	nd	lk	nk
sk	lp	mp	sp
ct	ft	lt	nt
pt	st	xt	lf

Triple consonant endings

nch	lth

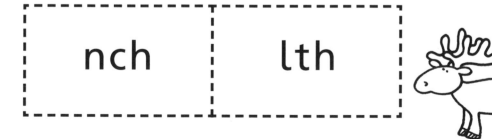

Resource sheet C

Initial consonant blends

bl	br	cl	cr	dr
dw	fl	fr	gl	gr
pl	pr	sc	sk	sl
sm	sn	sp	st	sw
tr	tw			

scr	spl	spr	squ
str	thr	shr	

Notes for teachers on Resource sheet D

Note that a phoneme is a sound made by a letter or a blend of letters. So the phoneme **ee** can be made by: **ee** as in the word feet; **ea** as in the word eat; **i** as in the word ski; **e_e** as in the name Pete; **y** as in the name Mary; etc.

At this stage we are looking only at **ee** and **ea**.

The phoneme **ai** can be made by: **ai** as in the word rain; **a_e** as in the word same; **ay** as in the word day; **ey** as in the word they; **ei** as in the word rein; **eig** as in the word reign; **eigh** as in the word weigh etc.

At this stage we are looking only at **ai**, **a_e** and **ay**.

The phoneme **ie** can be made by: **ie** as in the word tie; **i_e** as in the word kite; **igh** as in the word high; **y** as in the word fly; **ig** as in the word sign etc.

At this stage we are looking only at **ie**, **i_e**, **igh** and **y**.

The phoneme **oa** can be made by: **oa** as in the word boat; **o_e** as in the word hole; **ow** as in the word throw; **ew** as in the word sew; **oe** as in the word hoe etc.

At this stage we are looking only at **oa**, **o_e** and **ow**.

The phoneme **oo** can be made by: **oo** as in the word soon; **u_e** as in the word tune (though notice that in most part of the country the phoneme has changed slightly); **ew** as in the word flew; **ue** as in the word glue; **o** as in the word do; **oe** as in the word shoe etc.

At this stage we are looking only at **oo**, **u_e**, **ew**, **ue**.

Note that the phoneme cards at the bottom of Resource Sheet D are spaced so that consonant tiles from Resource Sheet A can be placed in the gaps. For example, the consonant tile 'p' could be placed on the first phoneme card to make the word 'ape'. This demonstrates the phoneme **ai**.

Long vowel phonemes

ee	ea	ai	ay
ie	igh	y	oa
ow	oo	ew	ue

a		e	o		e
i		e	u		e

Brodie's Reading Test for High Frequency Words

The following story, Jill's Bad Day, contains 105 of the words suggested in the NLS for Years 1 and 2. It also contains 30 of the suggested high frequency words for Reception.

The story is printed once for the child to read, and once with 100 of the Year 1 and 2 target words in bold with a box next to them. This is for you to use as an assessment sheet to record the sight recognition of these high frequency words. We suggest that you simply mark the box for each word that is read correctly. Find the total number of correct words and this will provide you with a percentage score for the test. We suggest that you carry out this assessment twice during the school year, thus enabling you to make a judgement of each individual pupil's progress. You may wish to spread the assessment over two sessions.

Please note that some of the target words appear more than once but are only tested once.

Years 1 and 2 words that appear in the story.
(Those in brackets are not tested.)

were	because	took	one	want	should
lived	too	red	blue	people	make
(an)	out	ball	saw	may	his
old	first	three	bed	laugh	just
school	then	more	did	help	been
next	about	with	what	have	how
their	twenty	her	do	got	many
house	nine	boy	back	that	here
had	put	if	home	way	where
sister	door	could	made	take	would
called	ran	can't	very	some	over
who	down	new	another	(off)	by
ten	good	(be)	will	push	much
brother	girl	(so)	him	as	now
twelve	but	little	(us)	night	than
name	there	not	again	two	from
after	time	your	don't	them	last
came	when	must			

Years 1 and 2 words missing from the story.

half	jump	man	or	pull	these
has	love	once	our	seen	water
dig					

30 Reception high frequency words that appear in the story.

and	to	look	up	you	is
they	was	on	it	like	the
in	big	she	go	my	mum
a	he	play	me	I	yes
went	day	said	at	we	no

Pupil's sheet

Jill's bad day

Jill and Jack were twins. They lived in a village and went to an old school that was next to their house. They had a baby sister called Lily, who was ten months old, and a big brother who was twelve years old. His name was Ben.

Lily

Jack

Jill

Ben

Every day after breakfast their Gran came to look after Lily because their Mum went to school too. She was a teacher. Mum went out first and then, at about twenty minutes to nine, Jill and Jack put on their coats, went out through the door and ran down the road to school.

Now, Jill was usually a good girl but today was going to be different. There was no problem until play time, when Jill took a red ball out to play. She chose three more children to play with her, and then the trouble began. A boy, who was only in Year One, asked if he could play too.

"No you can't, it's my new ball," said Jill crossly.

Just then, Jack came up.

"Don't be so mean," he said. "Let the little boy play. Anyway it's not your ball, it must be mine because I had the red one. Your ball is blue. I saw it on your bed."

Jill did not know what to do so she went back home. Gran called Mum on the telephone and made Jill say she was very sorry.

"Another time I will let him play with us," said Jill. "I won't be mean again. I don't want to go back to school because people may laugh at me," she said.

"Don't worry," said Gran. "I will help you. I have got to go that way to take some letters to the post box. Off we go! You push Lily as far as the school."

That night Mum said that the two of them should make friends before bed time and Jill should give Jack his ball.

"Yes, we have made friends," said Jack.

"It has just been a bad day," sighed Jill, "I won't mind how many people play ball next time. Here is your red ball, Jack. Where would you like me to put it?"

"Over by my bag please," replied Jack.

"I feel much better now than I did at school," said Jill as she got up from the chair. "That is the very last time I stop being good!"

Mum just smiled.

(Jill did the wrong thing by going home. Remember it is not safe to go out of school on your own.)

Brodie's Reading Test for Medium Frequency Words

Teacher's record sheet

Name of pupil: _____ Date of test: _____

Date of birth: _____ Year group: _____ Percentage score: _____

Jill and Jack **were** ☐ twins. They **lived** ☐ in a village and went to an **old** ☐ **school** ☐ that was **next** ☐ to **their** ☐ **house** ☐. They **had** ☐ a baby **sister** ☐ **called** ☐ Lily, **who** ☐ was **ten** ☐ months old, and a big **brother** ☐ who was **twelve** ☐ years old. His **name** ☐ was Ben.

Every day **after** ☐ breakfast their Gran **came** ☐ to look after Lily **because** ☐ their Mum went to school **too** ☐. She was a teacher. Mum went **out** ☐ **first** ☐ and **then** ☐ at **about** ☐ **twenty** ☐ minutes to **nine** ☐ Jill and Jack **put** ☐ on their coats, went out through the **door** ☐ and **ran** ☐ **down** ☐ the road to school.

Now, Jill was usually a **good** ☐ **girl** ☐ **but** ☐ today was going to be different. **There** ☐ was no problem until play **time** ☐, **when** ☐ Jill **took** ☐ a **red** ☐ **ball** ☐ out to play. She chose **three** ☐ **more** ☐ children to play **with** ☐ **her** ☐, and then the trouble began.

A **boy** ☐, who was only in Year One, asked **if** ☐ he **could** ☐ play too.

"No you **can't** ☐, it's my **new** ☐ ball," said Jill crossly. Just then, Jack came up.

"Don't be so mean," he said. "Let the **little** ☐ boy play. Anyway it is **not** ☐ **your** ☐ ball, it **must** ☐ be mine because I had the red **one** ☐. Your ball is **blue** ☐. I **saw** ☐ it on your **bed** ☐."

Jill **did** ☐ not know **what** ☐ to **do** ☐ so she went **back** ☐ **home** ☐.

Gran called Mum on the telephone and **made** ☐ Jill say she was **very** ☐ sorry.

"**Another** ☐ time I **will** ☐ let **him** ☐ play with us," said Jill. "I won't be mean **again** ☐. I **don't** ☐ **want** ☐ to go back to school because **people** ☐ **may** ☐ **laugh** ☐ at me," she said.

"Don't worry," said Gran. I will **help** ☐ you. I **have** ☐ **got** ☐ to go **that** ☐ **way** ☐ to **take** ☐ **some** ☐ letters to the post box. Off we go! You **push** ☐ Lily **as** ☐ far as the school."

That **night** ☐ Mum said that the **two** ☐ of **them** ☐ **should** ☐ **make** ☐ friends before bed time and Jill should give Jack **his** ☐ ball.

"Yes, we have made friends," said Jack.

"It has **just** ☐ **been** ☐ a bad day," sighed Jill, "I won't mind **how** ☐ **many** ☐ people play ball next time. **Here** ☐ is your red ball, Jack. **Where** ☐ **would** ☐ you like me to put it?"

"**Over** ☐ **by** ☐ my bag please," replied Jack.

"I feel **much** ☐ better **now** ☐ **than** ☐ I did at school," said Jill as she got up **from** ☐ the chair. "That is the very **last** ☐ time I stop being good!"

Mum just smiled.

Notes for teachers

The final two sheets of this book are designed to be photocopied back to back then laminated.

- They consist of all the high frequency words specified in the NLS for Reception, Year 1 and Year 2, except for 'I', 'a', the pupils' own addresses and the address of the school.

- To ensure that every letter is represented by some words we have added the following words that are not included in the NLS High Frequency list: ear, every, kite, kettle, quiet, x-ray, zoo.

- We have also added the following words to ensure that pupils can complete the dictation exercises on Worksheets 44 to 46: ask asked bark book caterpillar hungry Jenny likes read reading teacher

Each child should be given a laminated copy. This will become a really useful resource to be used for 'dictionary' work and for general spelling help.